ACCEPTING THE
CHALLENGE
TO GOD'S GLORY

Copyright Case ID:1-13236423161

Paperback ISBN: 9781304227997

Hardcover ISBN: 9781304227744

DEDICATION TO MY WIFE, SHARRON

"Till the Twelfth of Never"

When I first met you some 57 years ago, I knew deep down myheart you would be an incredibly special part of my life. It is only by God's grace He granted me the blessing of spending these many years with you. Thank you for keeping me grounded in my faith and focused on authoring this book. I will love you.

"Till the Twelfth of Never"!

FOREWORD

On September 16, 1967, I watched a miracle take place as an eleven-year-old boy. The heavily favored Texas A&M football team was hosting SMU in a season opener on national TV. SMU's first-team quarterback had to leave the game after getting injured. Ines Perez, who only measured to be a mere 5 ft. 4 in., was SMU's backup quarterback. The bottom edge of the number 16 on his tucked-in jersey lined up with his waistline. In a keenly contested game, A&M scored a go-ahead touchdown with only 43 seconds left on the clock. The TV camera then zoomed in on the Aggie cadets kissing their dates to celebrate what they thought was a sure victory. After SMU's Jerry Levias returned the ensuing kickoff close to midfield and with time running out, Ines led the Mustangs down to A&M's 6-yard line with consecutive completed passes. And with just 9 seconds left on the clock, Ines threw a touchdown pass to Jerry in the back of the end zone to win the game!

The outcome of that football game and Ines's confident leadership mirrored the surprising upset victory by a small, fearless fellow named David against the giant Goliath. Like God's favor with David, God has always had his hand on Ines throughout his life. [OBJ]

My father, Hayden Fry, was Ines's head coach at SMU. Coach Fry believed in Ines and loved him like a son. Because of the opportunity Coach Fry gave Ines to play football at SMU, Ines graduated with a college degree in education. She became a successful teacher, coach, and ultimately, a school district athletic director. Like Coach Fry, his career involved molding the lives of young people.

I had the privilege of knowing Ines when he was a player on my father's SMU team and now as a wonderful friend. In July 2021, I invited Ines and his wife Sharron to my deceased mother's tribute in Plano, Texas. I asked Ines if he would give the closing prayer at the event, and he accepted. A day before the tribute, there appeared to be a new Covid variant going around in the area, and I was afraid it might impact the attendance at the event. So, I called Ines to inform him as he and Sharron had just left their home in Buda, Texas to drive up to Plano. When I warned him of the situation, Ines said, "Kelly, my vehicle does not do U-turns." Ines and Sharron arrived to participate and celebrate with many other friends who knew my mother. It was a double blessing that Ines was present to give a heart-felt prayer at the end, and no one who attended the event caught the virus. In my opinion, Ines Perez is a man of integrity who puts others first... and a man after God's heart.

Family Picture:

Top Row; Left to Right: Randy and Ronnie

Middle Row; Jay, Ines, and Sharrilyn

Front Row; Sharron and Sarah

INES PEREZ

The purpose of writing my life story is not only to encourage those who have, at one time or another, been told they are not big enough, good enough, or from the right "pedigree " but also to understand how Jesus Christ can be our source of strength throughout our lives and can accomplish anything in His name.

1945 was a significant year in world history, marked by the end of World War II and the fall of Nazi Germany and the Empire of Japan. Major events which occurred in 1945 include:

- USS Indianapolis is sunk by a Japanese submarine
- War in Europe ends May 7th
- Adolf Hitler and his wife of one day, Eva Braun, commit suicide
- Harry S. Truman becomes US President following the death of President Roosevelt
- Nuclear bombs dropped on Hiroshima and Nagasaki
- Japan surrendered on August 14
- Germany Concentration Camps liberated
- Yalta Agreement signed
- Germany is divided between Allied Occupation Forces
- The United Nations Charter creates United Nations

These events shaped the course of history not only for the world but for Hispanics and Blacks in Corpus Christi as well. Hispanics, Blacks, and Whites had fought side by side during the war but, at home, remained enemies. However, things slowly turned around for all of us. The younger generation saw things differently, and after returning from war, hate, and animosity towards each other slowly faded away. The separated water fountains in downtown Corpus Christi for Blacks and Hispanics were being removed, and relationships were improving.

My dad had experienced war firsthand in Mexico and was worried my older brothers, Abdon and Senen, would have to go to war as well. However, Abdon did not qualify for the military due to physical problems. Senen was drafted and served only for a few years without seeing any combat.

My father always preached respecting and helping others. Even though things were not particularly good for Hispanics, men like W. R. Reed and Jack Ryan, whom he worked for at Corpus Christi Brick and Lumber, positively impacted race relations. They were genuine, good, loving people. My dad respected both so much he would have done anything for them.

My dad wasnot tall, maybe five feet four inches, and my mom was even shorter, four feet eleven inches tall. My three older brothers, Abdon and Senen, were five feet five inches tall, and Marcos, the tallest of the family, was five feet seven inches tall. My sisters Carmen, Gloria, Patsy, and Cynthia are also in the family. Needless to say, none of them are very tall either.

Not being born into a tall family presented a few challenges for me, but somehow, God always made it possible for me to overcome them.

At the time of my birth, Mom and Dad had three sons: Abdon, Senen, Marcos, and one daughter, Carmen. We lived in an upstairs apartment with a small kitchen, three bedrooms, a dining area, and a nice backyard. Small businesses followed to our apartment: a café, a barber shop, and a dance hall. However, the best part about living at this location was the two theaters located remarkably close to the apartment. The Grande Theater was a couple of buildings from our apartment on the same side of the street, while the Melba Theater was just across the street from the Grande Theater. I was born on August 3, 1945, in this apartment,

After working at Corpus Christi Brick and Lumber for a period of time, Dad was promoted to supervisor. He worked there for fifty years before finally retiring and saving enough money to purchase his own home. Dad was very frugal with his money. He knew exactly what he was saving his money for and once he saw what he wanted and it was available, he went after it. My mom told us Dad would always tell her he would build her a big house close to the ocean. For some reason, he was intrigued by the ocean. I remember being with him the day before he died, and he asked me to take him to the lobby where he could see the ocean. He stared out the window, enjoying the view of the beautiful clear blue water for about 15 minutes, smiled, took a deep breath, and said, "Now that is beautiful". Then he asked me to take him back to his room.

God not only blessed him with a house not too far from the ocean but also made it possible for him to open a clothing store, which he operated from the first floor of our two-story house. It was truly a blessing for all of us, but more so for Mom because she finally had a house like she had dreamed about ever since she was a little girl.

When we moved to our new house on Artesian, I was four years old but just a few months from turning five. After loading the truck with some of our furniture, Senen and I rode on the back of the truck. Well, not having any seat belts and sitting at the very back end of the truck, any sudden stop would send either of us flying out of the truck.

We had already made a trip with me riding in the back of the truck, so Dad and the boys did not give it a second thought about me riding back there again. Dad reminded me to be careful and to hold on. However, as we turned from Leopard to Artesian Street with the second load, Dad had to make a quick stop, and I went flying out of the truck and landed on my back, hitting my head on the curb. I was extremely fortunate I did not fracture my skull. Praise God, he gave me a hard head. It was only by God's grace nothing really happened to me other than some scrapes on my back and scaring me half to death. I was checked by a doctor, and he confirmed that I did not have any severe injury to my head.

Mom and Dad had a big room upstairs with four windows at the front. Mom and Dad's bed was near the stairs, towards the back of the room. Carmen had a bed next to the windows in the same room where Mom and Dad slept. Gloria, who was just a couple of months old, slept with my grandmother in a room at the back of the house.

Abdon and Senen each had twin beds in the middle room. Located across from the twin's room was a small room where Marcos and I shared a twin bed until I was at least twelve. Dad finally bought bunk beds, so Marcos and I could not share a bed.

Naturally, I drew the short end of the stick and had to take the top bunk bed. I fell a couple of times, but other than my pride being bruised, nothing serious happened to me. To this day, I am still amazed I made it through the first thirteen years of my life. I was both falling and hitting my head or being scared by my brothers.

It was a great neighborhood with boys my age with whom I could play. Alfred Boyd, Fernando Rodríguez, Don Harrison, and I attended the same elementary and junior high. Bobby Tamez, who lived across the street, attended Cathedral, a Catholic school near us. As football teammates in middle school, we not only had a ton of fun playing together, but we had a good football team. After I was moved to quarterback, Alfred became one of my favorite receivers. Fernando was a good running back, and Don was an awesome defensive player.

Our team was not noticeably big except for Mark Ramos, who weighed over 300 pounds but could move surprisingly well because of his size. As a ball carrier, though, we always tried to avoid being tackled by him.

Well, the unthinkable finally happened. During one of our scrimmages, Fernando ran a power play up the middle, and as he tried to plant and make a cut to the outside, he slipped and landed in one of the bigger potholes.

On that day, it had rained for several hours, and every pothole we had in the field was full of water. As we called him, Nano landed face down, with Mark landing on top of him. Nano was fighting to get up, but with Mark on top of him, he could not do so. The whole team struggled to get Mark off him. We had to have two of our coaches help us get Mark off Nano. Poor Nano was gasping for air, his face covered in mud, and I am sure his back was hurting from having Mark on top of him. It took several minutes before he regained his composure and was able to say a few words. We did not know whether to laugh or cry. Some laughed but were quickly told by the coach to shut up. He said this was not a laughing matter; Fernando could have died. After a few weeks even Fernando was laughing about what happened to him. Mark, on the other hand, apologized every time he saw Fernando.

When I was in high school, Don, Alfred, and I played football, while Fernando chose to run track and play baseball. Bobby concentrated on his studies because he wanted to be a pharmacist. Bobby was very smart and liked to spend hours studying. He made a great living as a pharmacist.

Since injuries to my head had not killed me, I could have easily died of shock! The twins were always scaring me. I will never forget when the twins took me to the movies. I watched TV, enjoying one of my favorite westerns, when Abdon approached me and whispered, "Do you want to go to the movies"? I was thrilled, and of course, I could not wait to go to the movies. I was nine years old and really enjoyed going to the movies to watch Roy Rogers, Tarzan, Lash Larue, or Gene Autry movies. I thought the featured movie for that day was a Lash Larue, but I was about to find out differently.

Once inside the theater, we went straight to the concession stand, where they bought me some popcorn, a Coke, and candy. However, I could not help but notice several Frankenstein advertisements and pictures of him on the way to the concession stand. I questioned my brothers about the posters, but they kept telling me they were just promoting the movie, which would be showing soon.

As soon as we entered the house (the house is the seating area to watch a movie), the twins went straight to the front. I was in the first seat of the very first row, with the twins sitting next to me. The house was dark, and I could not see the stage, which was about ten feet away from me.

Suddenly, the screen lit up and I saw Frankenstein about ten feet away from me. It caught me off-guard! I jumped out of my seat; with my popcorn and coke flying everywhere. I was outside the theater before my brothers even knew what had happened. I ran all the way home and hid under the bed. For weeks, I had nightmares and would not sleep by myself. I would curl up with Marcos and not move a muscle.

My sister Gloria will tell you that I was so scared that I would not go anywhere without having someone with me. After that incident, I never let them take me to the movies again. I would not take any chances of them repeating anything like that ever again.

A few months later, I remember another time the twins scared me. When I got up late at night to go to the bathroom, Abdon had placed a chair in the middle of the bathroom and was standing on it with a rope around his neck as he had hung himself. As I stepped into the bathroom Senen turned on the light and screamed, "Look!" as he pointed to Abdon. Without hesitation, I turned, and I honestly do not remember whether I ran or flew back to my bed! One thing for sure, I did not use the bathroom late at night without making sure all the lights were on and Abdon and Senen were asleep.

In 1958, before my thirteenth birthday, my dad wanted to visit his dying father. We did not have a car Dad considered roadworthy to make the long trip to Mexico, so he decided to purchase a new 1958 four-door Ford Fairlane 500. It was a beautiful black car. The morning after my brothers brought the car home, my dad, mother, sisters Gloria and Patsy, and my brother Marcos and I left for Guadalajara, Mexico.

Every time we stopped, Marcos and I polished the car. We wanted it to look just like it did when we left home. On the first day of our travel, we made it as far as Monterrey, Mexico, where we spent the night.

The next morning, Dad found a bakery around the corner from the hotel and bought some donuts, sweet bread, milk, and coffee, and off we went. Dad, Mom, Gloria, and Patsy were in the front seat. Gloria was on Mom's lap, and Patsy was sitting between my mom and dad, who was driving. Once we finished eating, I guess most of us decided to take a nap. I am not sure how close we were to reaching San Luis Potosi, but I knew we were getting close because Dad mentioned stopping at the next town in a few minutes.

As we approached a curve, an eighteen-wheeler came around the corner, taking up both lanes of the highway and forcing us off the road. I remember the car skidding and starting to flip sideways. Later, we discovered that we had flipped several times over a cliff.

The next thing I remember, I was suspended in the air and held by someone. As I turned my head to see who was holding me, I saw a beautiful bright light, but I could not see His radiant face. I heard His voice gently say to me, "**you are not finished.**" Then, I looked down to see my brother pulling me out of the car. My head was covered in blood, so Marcos took off his new shirt, wrapped it around my head, and held me. I saw my dad slapping my mother trying to keep her awake while my two sisters watched. They were so brave. Neither one of them cried.

Even though Gloria had a big hole in her armpit, she never complained. She just stood there watching everything go on. Patsy also just stood there witnessing everything taking place. I cannot imagine what was going through their minds, but they sure were strong.

The next thing I saw was a man running down the cliff to check on us and asking Marcos if he could help us. I am not clear on how we ended up in this man's car, but I remember waking up for just a minute or so in somebody's car and my sister Gloria proudly showing me the hole in her armpit. As soon as I saw the hole, I passed out and did not regain consciousness until the doctor inserted the first of 13 stitches in my head. I can honestly say I felt every single one of them! My sister told me later that my screaming frightened her. She told me she tried to hide her injury, but it did not work. She also received stitches. Praise the Lord, my younger sister Patsy walked away with minor scratches, while my brother Marcos had no injuries.

Later I found out my mom was treated for cracked ribs. I also learned the police took my dad and locked him up. For some crazy reason, the police arrested him, thinking he was trying to kill us. It was not until Marcos explained what had happened that they released him.

At some point, while they were stitching me up, I once again felt the presence of our Lord Jesus Christ in the surgery room. I cannot explain it, but serving my Lord Jesus Christ became a priority from that day forward.

When we returned to Corpus Christi, I started going to

church regularly and even attended a Catechism class at Sacred Heart Church.

In Catechism class, Sister Mary would have us memorize and recite scriptures from the New Testament in front of the class. The one who could memorize the most won a genuinely nice Blue cross with Jesus on the cross. I won the cross for memorizing more scriptures than anyone else.

Psalms 28:7 is one of my favorites.

"The Lord is my strength and my shield; my heart trusts in him, and he helps me. My heart leaps for joy and with my song I praise him." (NIV)

The Lord Jesus went through so much for us that nothing we go through can ever compare to His suffering. The pain I was experiencing was nothing I could not endure. He is the strength that keeps us motivated to accomplish anything we put our minds and hearts to.

No doubt God had a plan for me and kept me safe during all the falls and scares. He loves us so much. He will always be there to protect us! Scripture tells us, "For God so loved the world that he gave His one and only Son that whoever believes in him shall not perish but have eternal life." John 3:16 (NIV)

This verse is often considered the love verse of the Bible and defines the great love God has for us. I pray everyone I have ever been in contact with, after becoming a Christian, will testify I am truly a child of God.

My dad, a naturalized U.S. citizen, was immensely proud to be an American, and he preached to us that in America, we could be anything we wanted to be if we worked hard enough. He would tell us that a strong work ethic was important, but education was the key to success in the United States. He was adamant about us pursuing the highest degree of education. As far as he was concerned education trumped over everything else. I know he is why Senen, Marcos, Carmen, Gloria, Patsy, and I became teachers and administrators while Abdon became an accountant.

My mother was a tremendous support to my dad and, without a doubt, a great mother to all of us kids. She was the disciplinarian and our fashion designer. I say this because she made sure our clothes were well coordinated. I remember one day I was planning to wear a blue shirt with red pants, green socks, and tennis shoes to school. Well, that did not sit well with her. She immediately ran to the closet, picked out a pair of blue jeans and white athletic socks, and told me to change.

I cannot forget our Friday meals. Mom would prepare fish, shrimp, salad, rice and beans, and the best enchiladas. It was like eating at a restaurant. Some of my friends loved coming over to eat on Fridays, and my mom would never turn any of them away. They were welcomed at the table like any family member.

All three of my brothers played football at Miller High School. The twins were linemen on the 1955 Quarter-finalist team. Marcos quarterbacked the 1958 team to the semi-finals, losing to Pasadena High School by one point. So, the twins wanted me to continue to pursue their dream of leading the Miller Bucs to a State Championship. However, I was overweight. I weighed more in the fourth grade than I did in my senior year in high school. I weighed one hundred and forty in the fourth grade and only one hundred and twenty-nine my senior year, and I was not the prototype-looking quarterback. However, seeing firsthand what Marcos had accomplished as a quarterback at Miller motivated me to become a quarterback, also. He and the twins encouraged me every step of the way.

I also believe being coached by Bill Hooper at Miller prepared me physically and mentally for high school football and the college game. Physically, he had me go through a plethora of throwing exercises while running sideways, back peddling, and full speed straight ahead. Whether it was running to our right, left, or backward, he wanted us to simulate those actions we would need for a game. Activities like circle drill, drop back drill, clock drill, bar drill, and scramble drill were incorporated into our daily practices.

I cannot tell you the number of hours I spent with Coach Hooper watching films of our opponents. During the season, I would meet with Coach Hooper to watch a film and go over the best plays to run against short yardage and other down-and-distance situations we would face during a game. Coach even broke the football field into five areas of attack so regardless of where we had the ball, I knew which play to run. You might say Coach Hooper was the first coach to come up with a two-minute offense being run the whole game. He wanted to run as many plays as possible.

In today's game, plays are mostly signaled from the sideline. As for us, our plays were not signaled from the sideline as I called all the plays. I must credit Coach Ragus for having that much confidence not only in his assistant coaches, but his players. In my opinion, great head coaches coach their assistant coaches and allow their assistants to coach the players. Also, I think great coaches are always eager to learn for the benefit of their team. Speaking of great coaches, I remember before one of our home games Coach Gordon Wood, head coach from Brownwood High School and one of the winningest coaches in Texas, attended our team meeting just to see how we prepared the team offensively for a game.

At our meeting on Monday, Coach Hooper told me Coach Wood was extremely impressed with our approach to preparing for a game and would implement the same procedure with his quarterbacks and team.

Having two ex-Baylor quarterbacks coach me certainly elevated my play at quarterback. For the longest time, Baylor had been known as quarterback "U." I was blessed to have been coached by two of the best: Coach Hooper at Miller and, of course, Hayden Fry at SMU.

Dad Margarito and Mom, Fermina Perez

Back row: Brother-in-law, Benny; Middle Row: Brother Marcos, Sister Gloria, Sister Patsy, and Sister Carmen.
Front Row: Marcos' wife Gloria, Ines, and my wife Sharron.

Ines Perez, Marcos Perez, Senen Perez & Abdon Perez

Ines's second grade picture

Watching my twin brothers play football influenced me to play football as well. Their dream and ambition were to someday play college football, and their dream became a reality when they played at Del Mar College.

When the twins were playing football for our middle school, the Northside Hurricanes, I was in the fourth grade. I made it a point to watch them practice every day. The Northside practice field was just a couple of houses down and across the street from us, so it was very convenient for me to cross the street to watch their workouts.

I really liked my brother's coach. After practice, Coach Nichols would play catch with me. I would throw passes to him until most of the players had showered and left the fieldhouse. He enjoyed having me around because he asked me to be their "mascot." He ordered a uniform just like the team wore and told me to wear it when they played because I would be going to the games with them. Now, I needed a helmet because the helmets they had were too big for me. So, I talked my dad into buying a helmet I had seen at H.E.B. It was a blue plastic helmet with one bar across the face. At first, my dad was not too keen on the idea, but after my mom talked to him, he broke down and purchased it for me.

During game days, the Northside Hurricanes team would drive to our elementary school to pick me up. My fourth-grade teacher was excited for me and without any hesitation, she would encourage me to change into my football uniform and wait for the team to arrive. The class also waited in anticipation. As soon as they saw the bus, the class started cheering and hollering for the Hurricanes.

Ines in the fourth grade

Bruno Torres–Guard

Inez Perez
Future Hurricane

27

It was one of the most memorable times of my life. Everyone made a big deal out of it. The atmosphere was like a pep rally, and it fired up the team.

My elementary school, Cheston Heath, did not offer tackle football until I was in the sixth grade. I was ready! I loved football and knew I could make the team. However, when I tried out, I was cut from the team because I was too small. My brothers did not play for Cheston Heath because football was not offered when they were there. All three of them, however, played for Coach Martin at George Evans.

I was heartbroken. I wanted to play football so badly! I cried all the way home. I went straight to my room and wondered if I would ever be able to play football like my brothers. I did not want my brothers to know I had not even been given a chance to try out. I knew that if they found out I was not even given the opportunity, they would be mad and have something to say to the coach (if you know what I mean). However, it did not take long for them to find out. The first thing, they wanted to know was how practice went. When I told them I was not even given an opportunity to try out for the team, they were ready to have a nice long talk with the coach. My dad discouraged them from going to see the coach. Instead, Dad told them to encourage me to try out at George Evans. The next day, I went to talk with Coach Martin about trying out at George Evans. In those days, they did not have any attendance restrictions so anyone could attend one school and play for another school. At first, Coach Martin was hesitant but after thinking about it, he said, why not let us do it?

My tryout to make the team was to tackle their best running back, Ed Garza, a 5-foot 8 inch, one hundred and fifty pounders. His nickname was "Gorilla." He was mature beyond his age and seemed to enjoy hurting people. When Coach announced I had to tackle him everyone else just looked at me and said, **Pobresito**, translated in Spanish, *you poor guy, get ready to get hurt!* He had already hurt a couple of his teammates, so they thought they were going to see someone else get hurt.

Coach Martin placed two big dummies 5 yards apart between the goal line and challenged me to tackle him. Well, here I was facing this giant of a back with a look of aggression. My eyes did not want to make contact with his eyes, and all I could hear was what the players were saying, Pobresito. My heart was pounding, and I wanted to turn and run away from him but as he started toward me, I closed my eyes and started to head in the direction of Ed's first fake, but I tripped and went in the opposite direction. As fate would have it, he faked back in my direction, and with my eyes closed and trying to regain my balance, he ran right into my arms for a perfect tackle. Everyone went nuts, and Coach was yelling great tackle; you are on the team, my boy! No one really knows what happened but that is ok. I made the team and enjoyed playing.

Singing has always been something I genuinely enjoyed. While in fourth grade, my homeroom teacher loved taking me from class to class so I could sing my two "Elvis" songs; **"You Ain't Nothing but A Hound Dog" and "Don't Be Cruel."** Elvis was my favorite singer and I worked hard to imitate him.

Sometimes in the evenings, I would spend hours listening and trying to imitate his voice. I even combed my hair like Elvis combed his hair. It did not matter that I was overweight, some of my classmates told me I looked and could sing like Elvis, and I enjoyed singing for them, so I kept singing his songs.

My seventh-grade year at Northside Junior High School was a pivotal year for me (must credit my brother Marcos for using the word pivotal; he uses it a lot). I played guard on the football team just like my twin brothers did during their junior high years. I did not really enjoy playing on the line because everyone I went against was twice my size. But since I was built like my twin brothers, I was destined to be a lineman as well. However, the Lord gave me the opportunity to play quarterback when our starting quarterback got hurt.

Coach Nichols knew I could throw the football because we had played catch many times when my brothers played for him in the ninth grade. So, without any hesitation, I was moved to quarterback. The rest is history! The journey began. Hence, my brother's dream of both Marcos and I playing quarterback for Miller High School was coming to fruition.

The idea of Marcos and I playing quarterback for the Miller Bucs came about because of some discrimination the twins experienced at Miller. In the 1950s, when my brothers were playing for the Bucs, Hispanics faced significant discrimination. There were certain areas of town where Hispanics were not welcomed; fortunately, that discrimination did not cause much discord among teammates with all the players. Nevertheless, there were a couple of players who still disrespected Hispanic teammates. When an Anglo lineman suggested a play that suggested play would be run. But when a Hispanic player suggested a play, it was ignored. Sometimes he was even told to shut up and take care of their own assignments.

So, my brothers took it upon themselves to make sure Marcos and I did not face the same discrimination. They wanted us to unify the team by listening to our teammates and respecting everyone on the team. However, they wanted us to be the sounding voice in the huddle. They promised me I would not be a lineman.

I am a happy camper! Now, I would enjoy playing football a little bit more. I have always admired my linemen. They are truly the heart and soul of a team.

The work, and I mean work, began! My brothers started taking me to Miller High School, where they would have me run sprints and stadiums and do chin-ups. I started the workout by jogging a lap around the track followed by running twenty-yard sprints, then running ten stadiums. The truth is, I walked most of the ten stadiums at the beginning. After the stadiums, I walked another lap and finished with ten-yard sprints.

After the running workout, we would go to the chinning bar. The first time we went to the chinning bar, Abdon got this brilliant idea to put a neck harness around my neck and let me hang for a couple of minutes; I might grow a couple of inches. Senen was to hold me up and gradually let go of me, while Abdon held the neck harness to my neck, but as soon as Senen started to let go of me. I felt such excruciating pain in my neck, that I screamed bloody murder. They quickly took the harness off me and without missing a beat Abdon said, with a smile on his face, "I do believe you grew half an inch." If only looks could kill!

INEZ PEREZ

Ines's football program picture as a junior

After that ordeal, I did a combination of chins and arm hangs three times for ten seconds each until I gradually was able to hang for a minute. Eventually, I could move up to three sets of ten pull-ups without any problem. No, I did not enjoy it, and yes, I had a couple of choice words I shouted at them, but after slapping me behind my head, I learned not to say a word! Since Abdon and Senen were identical twins and their minds functioned the same way? They would both, in unison, say with a smile, "You will thank us later."

From the time I had my out-of-body experience after our wreck in Mexico, Jesus Christ became a big part of my life. He has been and will always be my Lord and Savior! He has never forsaken me, nor has He ever left me. There were a few times when my brothers were working me out that I felt like quitting, but His voice kept playing in my mind, you are not finished yet. And as I look back throughout my playing days at SMU, I remember at one point talking to Iowa State about transferring. However, I can honestly say God told me I still had a job to finish at SMU.

Garland Defeats Bucs for State Crown

(picture) Alfred Boyd making a "crucial" reception against the Spring Branch "Bears" in a Semi-Final football game

Garland beats us (Bucs) the following week for the State Championship

I pray young athletes who read this book will be encouraged never to give up, regardless of the odds against them.

My dad helped me by putting up a light pole in the backyard so I could use the light and practice late into the night. I spent many hours practicing. Looking back, the work my brothers put me through and the hours I practiced independently were well worth it.

It was not until my senior year that I realized my brothers were right to push me. All three of them played for some great coaches, and they learned what was required to play at an elevated level and did their best to pass it on to me. Each one of them helped me so much; I will forever be grateful to them.

I also credit my dad for all his support. I did not know it at the time, but my dad was a particularly good soccer player in Mexico. He loved sports and encouraged us to work hard to excel in whatever sport we played. Not only did my dad make suggestions pertaining to our physical training but he was continually active in his support. He purchased a trampoline so we could work on our balance and flexibility.

I consistently repeated the same workout for a few years. After supper, I would go into the backyard and work on ball-handling drills, faking, and throwing the football.

My three sisters (Carmen, Gloria, and Patsy) also played a vital role in my development. They were either my tackling dummies, played catch with me, or pushed me to work a little harder. I am immensely proud of all three of them. Carmen and Patsy, after influencing many young lives, recently retired from teaching and are enjoying spending time with their families. Gloria is the Hispanic Ministries and Global Missions Coordinator for the Austin Oaks Church in Austin.

My quarterback skills did not develop fully until my ninth-grade year. By then, I felt confident that I could lead the Miller Bucs to a championship. However, a big challenge was coming.

The "Big" challenge came when the head football coach of the Miller Bucs came to our middle school to talk to us about carrying on the Buc tradition and the big responsibility we would shoulder. I do not remember all he said because I was in "awe" of him. He was not only a great human being but also a great motivator.

I distinctly recall him reminding me of my three brothers who played on playoff teams while at Miller. Then suddenly, with this intense look on his face, looking at me and asking, are you going to help Miller win or be the "Black sheep" of the family?

Not knowing what he meant, I asked my brothers what Coach meant by that question. Marcos explained it to me. He explained that Coach was challenging me to represent our family as well as they had.

James 1:2-4, "Consider it pure joy, my brothers, and sisters, whenever you face trials of many kinds, because you know that the testing of your faith produces perseverance. Let perseverance finish its work so you may be mature and complete,not lacking anything." (NIV)

The next day, I started lifting and working on my quarterback skills even more. My best friend, Alfred Boyd helped me with my weight-lifting technique so I could get stronger. Alfred was built like a Greek god and strong as a bull. He would come to the house and use the weights my brothers had made from different-sized cans filled with cement. He and I spent quite a bit of time working on pass routes until both of us were exhausted. It paid off in the playoffs which I will explain later.

Ines Perez scampers for the third touchdown against the Alice Coyotes.

Buccaneers Smother Coyotes 47-0

Ines scoring a touchdown against the Alice
"Coyotes"

During our sophomore and junior years at Miller, we had winning seasons, but it was not until my senior year that our team was gifted with talent. We had talent and size except for me and our starting guard, Joe Marquez. He was an inch shorter than I was but as tough and aggressive as any player we had or played against.

Dave Campbell's Magazine had us #1 in the state going into our first ball game. We played up to our ranking by beating Alice 47-0, San Antonio Alamo Heights 32-0, and San Antonio Jefferson 19-0. In the fourth game of the season, we traveled to Odessa to play the Permian Panthers.

For the first time in our playing careers, we experienced a very hostile environment. At the stadium, our bench was so close to the stands that we had to keep our helmets on the whole time because bottles and other objects were being thrown at us. I am unsure if that had anything to do with our performance, but Odessa beat us 23-14.

We recovered the next week by beating a highly rated Galveston team. Then, we proceeded to beat Dallas Jesuit 58-0, Carroll Tigers 18-6, and San Antonio Brackenridge 40-27. At one point, Brackenridge was ahead 14-0 in the first two minutes of play, and that was before we even gained a first down.

In our next-to-last game, we beat Victoria, 8-6. Lee Spears, our running back, and defensive safety made a tackle at the one-yard line to preserve the win. Our final game of the season was against our rivals Corpus Christi W. B. Ray. Our win against them was secured by a great catch made by Gary Alexander. It snapped a 2-year reign as Zone Champions by the Texans. It was one of the most satisfying wins for all the seniors.

I still remember calling the throwback pass to Gary and seeing him outrun the defensive back into the end zone. Earlier in the game, Coach Hooper had told me that when I sprinted to the right, the defensive back away from the ball was not paying much attention to the backside receiver. I decided to test him. We were in a third-down situation with the score tied late in the game.

The ball was on our left hash mark, so I would sprint to the right and hopefully get their right defensive back to lean more toward the middle of the field. In the huddle, I told Gary to stick to the sideline on his route. He ran his route to perfection. Sure enough, the defensive back kept his eyes on me and favored the wide (left) side of the field. This allowed Gary to run right by him. Gary caught the ball in full stride for a 70-yard touchdown.

Ray played great defense all game and had stopped our high-powered offense consistently throughout the ball game. It was truly a classic and typical knockdown Miller vs Ray brawl.

Our win snapped a 2-year reign as Zone Champions by the W.B. Ray Texans. It was one of the most satisfying wins for all the seniors. We were so excited about winning the game we carried the coaches into the shower and enjoyed the victory together.

Takes seven guys to get James down.

Ines be nimble, Ines be quick, he jumped clear over the pile.

Ines is running for a first down against Kingsville in a Bi- District game

In my senior year, our first playoff game was against Kingsville High School; however, it was not under normal circumstances. The game was scheduled for Friday, November 22. We did not know it then, but we were all about to live through a world-changing event. One that I honestly believe brought a moral decline to our country. President John Kennedy was assassinated in Dallas, Texas, at around 12:30 pm Central Standard Time. President Kennedy was pronounced dead 30 minutes after the shooting. When it was announced over the PA system that our President had died, I could hear wailing all over the halls of our school. Students, teachers, and administrators were in shock. Playing a football game was the furthest thing from our minds. To tell you the truth, some of our players, including myself, did not feel much like playing the game. In fact, I would not have minded it if the game were postponed. However, after district administrators from Kingsville and Corpus Christi met, it was decided that playing the game might benefit our communities and players. So that night, we played Kingsville and beat those 35-9.

Our offense during the playoffs was very productive. If we were not moving the ball on the ground, our passing game was very proficient and helped us put points on the scoreboard. Sometimes, when our offense clicked on all cylinders, we were extremely hard to stop. Winning by twenty or more points was not out of reach for us. On the other hand, our defense was now very parsimonious and hard to score on.

Stalwart play by our defensive team, composed of Roger Muniz, Hal Carew, Raul Ortiz, Carlos Gonzales, Lee Spears, Eddie Valdez, James Pullam, Jesse Weatherby, Demitrio Morales, Anthony Hill, and Margarito Guerrero, played a major part in our advance into the State Championship game. We had a couple of other close calls a few games later. The game, I remember, was against an exceptionally talented Robert E Lee team from

San Antonio. They had big, strong linemen and, from what was said in San Antonio, the best back in the State(along with Warren Mcvea), Linus Baer. We won a thriller 21-19 but had to have a great defensive play towards the end of the game to preserve the win.

Lee was driving the ball at will and got to the 25-yard line. With less than a minute and a half to go in the game, their quarterback took the snap and scrambled around until he spotted an open receiver around the 15-yard line (they had an excellent field goal kicker). I just knew that he would complete the pass, set them up for a field goal, and win the game. However, out of nowhere, one of our safeties broke in front of their receiver and intercepted the ball to preserve the win. We ran out the clock and won the game!

After our win against Lee, we had to play another team loaded with tons of talent. Spring Branch High School had some Division I linemen and a running back who signed with the University of Texas Chris Gilbert. We played this game in the afternoon (our first) in the mud at their home stadium. This game was our best game of the season. We dominated the game both offensively and defensively. The score did not truly show our dominance, but our defense stopped them cold, and we ran pretty much at will on offense.

As I pointed out earlier, Alfred and I worked out a lot together. During practice we often communicated in Spanish about what type of pass route he would run. During the Spring Branch game our offense was facing a third and long situation. This was late in the game, and the score was close, 7-6. I called a pass play in the huddle, which did not include Alfred. He was to stay in for maximum protection. When I got under the center, I saw the linebackers creeping up to the line of scrimmage, ready to *blitz, so I yelled in Spanish to Alfred, "I need you over the middle quick."* He ran what we called a perfect 'hot' route, and I hit him in stride. He gained 15 yards for a first down. This was the deciding drive that won the game for us 14-6. Many considered our game against Spring Branch our "Championship game." We played an almost perfect match.

JAKE TRUSSELL AWARD
for the
Most Valuable High School Football Player
in South Texas for 1963

INES PEREZ
of the
ROY MILLER BUCCANEERS

Selected by the sports editor of the Kingsville Record for being "the high school football player who, through his all-around ability and team leadership, contributed more to the success of his high school football team than any other player in South Texas."

Playing for the State Championship was nothing new for Miller High School. In 1960 the "Bucs" won the Title against Wichita Falls, and our fans were noticeably confident we would bring home the "Championship Trophy."

We went into the game favored to beat Garland High School. However, we did not play our best game, and the freezing weather did not help us. But let us not take anything away from Garland. They were talented and extremely well-coached. They beat us 17-0.

Chuck Curtis was their coach. The following year, he coached Garland to another State Championship. Sometime later, he joined the SMU staff while I played at SMU.

Once our season was over, we saw college coaches visiting some of our players. We had some exceptionally talented players, some played Division I football. Gary Alexander, receiver, and Raul Ortiz, linebacker/wingback, went to Baylor, and James Spears, our fullback, went to Kansas. A couple of our players, Alfred Boyd and Hal Carew committed to play at Henderson County Junior College. Our center, Chuck Fuqua, decided on Wharton Junior College. Lee Spears, our running back/safety, also received a full scholarship as well. I accepted a four-year scholarship to Texas A & I University, but during a summer practice, I took a direct hit to my head, and for days, my vision was blurry. It was also hard for me to concentrate. Finally, I went to the doctor and was told that continuing to play football would not be wise. I was told that I had suffered a concussion, and since I had already been through a traumatic head injury at an early age, I could lose my life if I took another hit to the head.

I hated hearing what the doctor had to say. However, telling Coach Steinke was even more difficult for me. My coach said my full scholarship would be reduced to a half-semester basis if I remained as a team manager. I could not believe what I was hearing. I did not want to be a manager; I wanted to play football. So, I went home and told my dad and brothers.

My brothers were not happy with what I told them. My dad, on the other hand, was glad I might not be playing any more football for fear I could get seriously hurt. To appease me, he offered to pay for my education if I stayed at home and attended the nearby junior college. All three of my brothers, Abdon, Senen, and Marcos, had at one time attended and played football for Del Mar Junior College before football was suspended due to the lack of funding.

The twins played for Del Mar when they played in the Industrial Bowl against Henderson County Junior College. One of the players, Leon Spencer, who played against them in that game, later became a coach and Director of Athletics for Henderson County when I played for Henderson County. Marcos played quarterback for Del Mar in 1959 when they played in the Junior Rose Bowl in Pasadena, California.

It would have been very convenient for me to attend Del Mar because it was just a few blocks from where we lived. However, my heart was still set on playing football. My mind kept going back to what I heard my Lord and Savior Jesus Christ saying to me, "you are not finished yet." I was not ready to give up on my dream and felt God still had a bigger plan in store for me.

Ines receiving the 1963 "Jake Trussell Award" for
the MostValuable Football Player in South Texas

The thought of my football career being over was devastating. A few days later, I called my best friend, Alfred Boyd, and told him what had happened. I asked about their quarterback situation. It did not take Alfred a second to let me know their quarterback had broken his arm and they needed a quarterback. He asked if I would be interested in playing for Henderson County. Of course, I said yes. I immediately called the Head Coach, Tommy Steigleder. He told me to come; he had a scholarship for me. He told me he would have someone pick me up at the airport in Corpus Christi the next day, which was Thursday. For me to be eligible, I had to play at least one play on that Saturday against Kilgore Junior College.

The next day, one of the doctors from Athens flew to Corpus to pick me up. The funny thing was when he arrived, I was sitting on a bench waiting for him near where the small planes park. He went right by me and asked inside about a young man with a suitcase waiting to be picked up. I guess someone inside told him I was outside waiting for someone from Athens to pick me up. He came back outside and asked me if I had seen a young man waiting to be taken to Athens to play football. When I told him I was the one he was to pick up, he looked surprised because, as he put it, "he was expecting someone taller." I told him I was expecting a bigger plane. Well, that broke the ice, we had a good laugh, boarded the plane, and took off.

Once we approached Athens, Dr. Jones decided to circle the practice field as the team went through their pre-game preparations. When we landed, he drove me to the practice field to meet Coach Steigleder and the team. I do not think the team was too impressed with me. In fact, the first assistant, Coach Baccarini, who became the head coach at the end of the season, was later quoted as saying he was surprised by my size and wondered if I could withstand the pounding. Doctor Jones later said he thought someone was playing a joke on him at the time.

For those small players aspiring to play college football, I encourage you to keep your faith and trust in Jesus Christ. He will always provide you with what you need to pursue your dream.

"Trust in the Lord with all of you heart and lean not on your own understanding, in all of your ways submit to Him and he will make your paths straight."

Proverbs 3: 5-6 (NIV)

The next Saturday, we got on a Charter bus to play Kilgore for the first time. As I mentioned earlier, to be eligible, I had to play one play, so Coach Steigleder put me in the game and had me run quarterback sneak. Since I had not practiced with the team and did not know the offense that was the extent of my playing that night. The following week I started and from then on, I played every down and every game. We had a winning season but did not play in a bowl game.

My sophomore year we went undefeated and were ranked number one in the nation after our third or fourth game. We had most of our players back from the previous year and signed some outstanding players to go with the returning players. However, we played a couple of outstanding teams who tested us.

Tri-Captains for the season were Jim Boller, Inez Perez, and Alfred Boyd.

Jim Boller, Ines Perez, and Alfred Boyd elected captains for the Henderson County Junior College Cardinals

Ines's sophomore year at Henderson County Junior
College

One team that tested us was Texarkana. We had to travel to play them in Texarkana in freezing rain. We lost the coin toss and had to receive against a strong wind. We received the kick-off only to lose the football to a vicious tackle. Our running back was hit so hard that the ball and helmet went in opposite directions. A couple of our players chased his helmet, thinking it was the football. Fortunately, he was okay but did not return to the ball game until the last few minutes of the fourth quarter. Texarkana scored before we had even played two minutes of the football game.

It reminded me of our high school game against Brackenridge from San Antonio. We received the opening kick-off only to fumble the ball on the game's very first play. Warren Mcvea scored on a 45-yard run the first time he touched the ball. On our second possession of the ball, we fumbled again on the first play, and once again, Warren Mcvea scored on a long run. So, with only two minutes gone in the game, we were behind 14-0. Coach Ragus and the rest of the staff never lost their poise or confidence in us. They calmly reminded us to stick to the game plan and execute it, and things would work out. I remember my brother Marcos coming over and saying some encouraging words to me which lifted my spirits. The only challenge Coach Ragus put in front of us was whether we would respond like "Champions" or be just another run of the mill team?

Well, as we received the ball for the third time and huddled up. I felt nothing but confidence in the huddle from my teammates. Buffalo (Margarito Guerrero, Alfred Boyd, and Little Joe Marquez) kept repeating, "We are Champions, we are not just another team." We were a different team after that. We executed to perfection. Our defense allowed only one more score, and at the half, we led Brackenridge 28-21. We went on to win the game 40-27. Now back to the Texarkana game.

After Texarkana scored, I felt confident we would bounce back and win the game, just like we did against Brackenridge in high school. Praise the Lord, we managed to recover and win the game, but it was not an easy game.

Another team that ranked high that year was Kilgore. We played them twice, and surprisingly, we controlled both games and won big. However, I took a hit to the head, which sent me to the dressing room prior to the end of the first half of the second game. I was hit hard enough to see stars. My teammates told me later I walked over to the Kilgore huddle after getting hit and started to call a play. However, they grabbed me and escorted me back to our huddle.

During the off-season, there was not much to do in Athens, so we had to create our own entertainment. One thing we learned from the older players was pulling the old "let us go visit the Susie girls. This was a yearly prank we played on the new recruits at Henderson County.

We would tell the recruits about a couple who lived outside of Athens and had 5 beautiful daughters who loved to entertain football players. However, we had to make sure their father, a truck driver and ex-Marine, was not at home because he would shoot anyone who came close to his daughters. Well, one weekend, when we had several recruits visiting, we planned to take these new recruits to visit the girls. Somehow, Coach Steigleder got wind of it and warned the team about taking the new recruits to see the girls.

We decided not to do it because we knew what the punishment would be, and the punishment would not be fun at all!!

Valentine's weekend of my first year, my friend Fernando Rodriguez, from Baylor University came to Athens to spend the weekend with me. As mentioned earlier, Fernando, Alfred, and I grew up together in Corpus Christi. You might say we were the "Three Amigos." It seems like we were always together when we were growing up. Very few times would you see one of us by ourselves. Our friends often suggested someone should initiate adoption procedures because we looked lost when we were not together.

Having Fernando visit us at Henerson County was special. We knew he had to borrow someone's car and save enough money for gas to get to Athens, so we wanted to really show him a fun time. We did not have nightclubs or inexpensive restaurants to take him to, and the walk-in movie was not cheap, so we took him to Dairy Queen and played a ton of cards. It must have been a very dull weekend for Fernando, but we enjoyed having him visit us.

On Sunday Alfred, Fernando, and I went to church with a group of guys from the team. Little did I know my life was going to change forever. I saw this beautiful girl I had never seen on campus before, and I knew at once that we were destined for each other.

Sounds crazy does it not, but that is what God had in store for me!

Since a few of my teammates knew some of the girls from the girl's dorm, we invited them, along with this beautiful girl, Sharron, to go to the convenience store for some snacks later in the day. Our cafeteria did not serve dinner on Sundays, so we were alone. After leaving the convenience store, I invited Sharron to sit with me on the steps of the Student Union. As we talked, I realized the more we talked, the more I fell in love with her. The next thing I knew, I told her I was going to marry her. Her response was, "You are crazy!"

When I told Alfred and Nano what I had said to Sharron about marrying her, they nodded their heads, laughed, and wished me luck. All three of us talked about someday living close enough to each other that we could play golf every day and even have our kids run around together.

Soon after, we started seeing each other on a regular basis. When summer came, though, we had to go our separate ways. Sharron moved back to Elkhart, Texas, and I went back home to Corpus Christi, Texas. After receiving letters from her for a couple of weeks, I decided I had to see her, so I drove 350 miles just to talk to her on the phone for about five minutes. Talking to her on the phone was not my goal, it just worked out that way. Her dad had her busy and could not leave the house. Somehow, knowing I was close to her made a difference.

The following year, my sophomore year, we had an awesome football team. We went undefeated and were invited to play in the Junior Rose Bowl, but at the time, we did not know who we would be playing. Word got to us that we would play the winner between Fullerton Junior College from Fullerton, California, and City College of San Francisco.

After an undefeated season, our team was invited to a Dallas Cowboys game against the Cleveland Browns. The game was played on November 21, 1965. It was an exciting game, but Jim Brown led the Browns to victory 24-17.

During the Cowboys game, we kept hearing about a player San Francisco had named O.J. Simpson. Word was he was the best running back in junior college and that we would be playing them in the Junior Rose Bowl. However, we found out that Fullerton had beaten City College so that Fullerton would be our opponent in the Junior Rose Bowl later that day.

We were ranked number one in the nation when we played Fullerton, but after losing 19-15, they ended up number one, and our team was the number two in the nation. I was blessed with a few honors after the season. I was named to the All-American team and voted Most Valuable Player in our Conference. I was not the only player to receive honors after the season. Also receiving All-American honors were Alfred Boyd, Hal Carew, Margarito Guerrero, Carlos Gonzales, and Margene Atkins

Sharron and I continue to get closer to each other and spent time together when we could. The thought of being away from her again was something I did not want to do. When I got home at the end of the semester,

I told my dad that I had decided to marry Sharron. He said, "Bring her home." Even though he had not met her, Dad trusted my judgement and was ready to welcome her with open arms. My mom, on the other hand, did not want to lose her baby boy. She cried but said it would be ok only if she and I would live with them. She wanted to get to know her, spend time with her, and help her make all my favorite foods.

Finally, on December 30, 1965, we got married. It was a simple wedding, and Alfred was my best man. Fernando was already away at college, so he could not attend. The three of us did plan to spend more time together after we all had a family, but as you grow older and have a family, priorities change.

Unfortunately, Fernando died at the age of 50 from a heart attack after running a mile or so in the hot Corpus Christi Sun. After finishing his run, a young lady who lived in the same apartment complex he lived in was walking by with her dog, and Fernando asked if he could pet her dog. When he bent over to pet the dog, he collapsed and died of a heart attack. It was a devastating loss for all of us. Fernando was such a fun, caring friend. Alfred, Bobby, and I were in shock, and of course, we still miss him a lot.

Coach Dave Smith signing Ines to SMU

After playing for the National Championship in the Junior Rose Bowl, several of our players were offered Division I scholarships. I visited and was offered a scholarship at Iowa State, but after stepping off the airplane into two feet of snow in April, Iowa State was not for me. Hal Carew had an outstanding career at the University of Miami. Alfred, Margarito, and Carlos also had great careers at Wichita State University. After leaving Wichita State, Margarito transferred to Texas A&I in Kingsville, Texas, where he earned All-American honors as a defensive tackle.

A couple of days after returning from my trip to Iowa, I received a call from SMU. Coach Hayden Fry offered me a scholarship, and I immediately accepted! A few days after talking to Coach Fry, Coach Smith, the offensive line coach, visited me at Henderson County, and I signed a full scholarship.

Playing for SMU was one of the most memorable experiences for me. Being coached by Coach Fry was such an honor. He was not only a football genius with the X's and O's but a great psychologist and an even greater father figure. He had a big heart and a smile bigger than Texas! How he managed to remember all his players,' players' wives,' and parents' names, I will never know, but he was always quick to call them out when someone came to visit him. He was and is still loved by many. He will never be forgotten!

As quarterback I was running second behind Mike Livingston who was the first team All-State quarterback the same year, I was third team All-State my senior year in high school. Mike was a gifted athlete, with lots of speed, and could throw the ball a country mile. After he graduated from SMU, he was drafted by the Kansas City Chiefs and helped them win a Super Bowl Championship. However, regardless of experience, size, or speed, Coach Fry was still up in the air about who would start at quarterback the 1966 season. His quotes in the paper mentioned all three of us having outstanding summer practices. Mac White and Mike Livingston had of course played the year before and had some impressive statistics. I, on the other hand, was the new kid on the block, having played only Junior College football, but did have some championship experience at all levels up to now.

Even though I had a great "fall" practice my first year at SMU, I knew our senior quarterback, Mac White, was going to be the starter. Being a returning starter, and being a true team leader, I had no problem with him leading the team.

Ines warming up prior to the start of the Junior Rose
Bowl football game

Inez passes an important one to Roosevelt Bonner.

Ines passes to Roosevelt Bonner at the Rose Bowl

During that first fall practice at SMU, I was having a good scrimmage. It was better than either I or others expected.

I remember the first time I carried the football in our scrimmage. I was rolling to my right, and out of nowhere, our All-American nose tackle, John LaGrone, met me just as I cut up-field for what I thought would be a big gain. However, he hit my head on, and I can honestly tell you I had never been hit that hard. He drove me back 5 to 10 yards and knocked me on my back. I thought I had been run over by a Mack truck. John stood over me, smiled, and said, "Welcome to the Southwest Conference." After that play, I decided I would not cut across the grain; I would just stick to the sidelines. Other than taking the big hit from John, overall, I had a good scrimmage. I completed six of nine passes with 2 touchdowns, and I ran for 22 yards and a score.

For the rest of fall practice, coaches focused primarily on preparing for our first game against the Illinois "Fighting Illini." I did not get many reps after our scrimmage and the starting quarterback was going to be Mac White, which was, without a doubt, the right decision. We won the game against Illinois. I played a few plays during the season, but the most important thing was Mac led us to the Southwest Conference Title and the opportunity to play Georgia in the Cotton Bowl. Georgia won the game, but it was still an unbelievable experience.

During the spring, I tried out for the baseball team and was able to perform well enough to make the roster. I had not played baseball in two years since Henderson County Junior College did not have a baseball program. I was a little rusty. In high school, I helped pitch our team to the regional finals but did not try to pitch at SMU. In high school, I also played in the outfield when I was not pitching, so I felt surprisingly good about my chances of playing in the outfield. I remember the first time I started in the outfield against the Texas Longhorns. I had a good warm-up practice and was ready to play my first college baseball game. We finished warm-up, and we all gathered in the dugout for a pep talk by Coach Finley. Coach Finley chewed a few packs of Red Man tobacco each game, and so did a couple of our players. I was the only outfielder who did not chew and was being challenged by some teammates to try it. Well, I, being the good teammate I was, decided to join them. That day, the heat must have been a hundred. It did not take long for me to get extremely dizzy. By the time we went out to start the game, I was green in the face and could not see straight. As fate would have it, the first batter hit a shot between Mike, our center fielder, and me. I never saw it, but I could hear Mike yelling at me to chase the ball. Coach Finley and Mike were terribly upset with me, to say the least. When I got to the bench after the inning was over, I threw up all over the dugout. Players were bailing out so fast you would have thought the dugout was on fire. I finished the game on the bench and never chewed again!!! I started at left field the rest of the season and had a good year.

Rolex Watch players and coaches received for
playing inthe 1967 Cotton Bowl Classic against the
Georgia "Bulldogs"

1966 Championship Ring for winning the
Southwest Conference

We had some talented players on the baseball team. Donnie Denbow, our third baseman, was drafted by the Dodgers, and we had a pitcher who went on to play some pro ball as well. Anyway, we ended somewhere towards the bottom of the pack but not last. Texas, of course, and the Texas A&M Aggies were the big guns. Texas had great pitching and some heavy hitters, and the Aggies were also loaded with some great hitters.

During the summer of my senior year, a couple of our starting linemen and I would get together in the mornings. We would run stadiums, do some laps, and play several handball games. My brother Marcos had taught me how to play handball at the "Y" in Corpus Christi. He was very well known as one of the top players in South Texas and competed in several big tournaments. He either won or placed exceedingly high in all the tournaments he competed in. I believe playing handball helped me tremendously with my quickness, coordination, and mental toughness.

In the afternoons, Jerry Levias and I would often work on our routes and a route we called "Squirrel In," where he goes to the corner of the end zone and waits for the ball but not really knowing if it is going to be an out or some kind of curl. Most of the time, I would scramble a little, and then throw the ball towards the back of the end zone. He would jump and make some unbelievable catches. It was so much fun watching him make these fantastic catches! Little did we know this play, our "Squirrel In," would be the last play of the game which would beat the Texas A&M Aggies.

Well, fall practice started, and again, I had a good, solid performance, but Mike Livingston was to be the starting quarterback, with me being the backup. Any competitor wants to be the starter, and naturally, I want to be the one to start. I could taste it. However, I knew Mike had waited for his turn, and without a doubt, he was an excellent choice. I was not mistreated, lied to, or given false hope. Coach Fry was always straightforward with us, and we knew where we stood. Coach Fry told me to stay ready, though, because if something happened to Mike, I would be the next one going in.

Well, the season was about to start. We were to play a conference game against Texas A&M on national TV. This was the first time the football season was to open with a conference football game on national TV. Some said that it was because SMU had the first Black athlete to play in the Southwest Conference. Regardless of the reason, we were all excited to be playing on national TV. I do not remember Coach Fry saying anything about it other than we would be seen by our "Mammas and Poppas."

The night before the ball game, after we had our supper and team meeting, Coach Fry, Jerry, and I shot some pool. I cannot say any of us could take on Rudoff Wanderone, known as New York Fats, a well-renowned pool player, but we enjoyed playing. We did not play long because our bed check was getting close. However, it helped us relax and took our minds off the game for a little while.

Afterward, Jerry reminded me to say my prayers. He is

a strong Christian brother with a deep love for Jesus Christ. God's word has always brought comfort and peace to my life and spending time with our Lord Jesus Christ was something I wanted to do that night.

I read from **Psalms 34:4,** "I sought the Lord, and he answered me; he delivered me from all my fears." (NIV)

I was not fearful of getting hurt; nothing like that had ever entered my mind. For the first time in my career, I felt a big responsibility to my high school, all the young Hispanics who might be watching, and, of course, my family. This would be the first time my dad would have the chance to see me play a college game, which is if the opportunity presented itself. Also, given my size, this might be my only opportunity for other small athletes to take courage and have confidence they could someday play in the Southwest Conference.

That Night, I visualized myself in the game, throwing completed passes to my receivers. I did not see who the receivers were, but one of them caught the winning touchdown pass. I saw our team celebrating a victory.

Ziz Ziglar wrote about "Positive Thinking" and "As a Man Thinketh;" which I considered incredibly good motivational quotes, but the quote I had written on an index card and carried with me in my wallet was from scripture.

"For I know the plans I have for you declares the Lord, plans to prosper you and not to harm you, plans to give you hope and a future." Jeremiah 29:11 (NIV)

My brothers always encouraged me to see myself as a winner. They never said anything negative or derogatory to make me feel inferior. Zig Ziglar has a quote to that effect: "If you don't see yourself as a winner, then you cannot perform as a winner."

The morning of our game, we had a nice pre-game meal of steak, eggs, and some fruit. I normally do not have any problem eating all my food, but for some reason, that day was different. I felt overly excited and anxious about the game. However, once we arrived at the stadium, I was just as calm and poised as I had ever been.

As the bus turned the corner toward the stadium, we saw the Corps of Cadets lined up and ready to march into the stadium. It presented a problem for us because they blocked our path to our dressing room. I am not sure if it was a tradition or just a rumor, but some of our players were saying that if we tried to walk through their ranks, they would fight. We had no choice but to walk right through their ranks. Some of the Aggie Corps made an aggressive move towards us but when they saw that we would not be intimidated, they made room for the team to walk freely through to the dressing room.

One of the biggest disappointments for me and my family in Corpus Christi was not being introduced to the seniors before the beginning of the game. I was never told seniors were going to be introduced. One of my teammates mentioned it to me as we ran to the field for the start of the game. My thought was that only starting seniors were introduced, so I did not let it bother me.

The first quarter was like a boxing match. Both teams exchanged blows, and each scored a touchdown. In the second quarter, we kicked a field goal to go ahead 10-7 at the half. The sad news, we found out, was Mike Livingston had injured his knee on the last play and it was very doubtful he would be able to play in the second half. The team physician, Doctor Morgan, informed Coach Fry that Mike would not be able to play the second half. I was sitting by Jerry when Coach came over and said, "Well, Cowboy, you're going to ride this horse some the second half," winked, smiled, and walked away. However, Mike started the second half, but reinjured his knee. So, I got my chance to quarterback our team.

After the Aggies had tied the game early in the third quarter, we took the ball and quickly drove to the Aggie 15-yard line. The big play on that drive was a 16-yard pass to Mike Richardson. Dennis Partee kicked a field goal to put us back into the lead 13-10. The Aggies, however, were not going to be denied. Their outstanding quarterback, Edd Hargett, was razor sharp with his passing, connecting with Tommy Maxwell twice for 12 and 17 yards, Jimmy Adams for 16, and Ross Brupbacher for 15. With 43 seconds left in the game, Hargett hit Bob Long in the end zone to take the lead 17-13. With only 43 seconds left, no one expected us to win the game.

As I looked up in the stands. I saw all these Aggie Cadets kissing their girlfriends. They just knew victory was on their side. I smiled and waited for us to receive the kickoff. Little did we know, God had a bigger plan none of us knew about.

The kickoff went to Jerry, and he ran the ball to the 42-yard line. The "Miracle" began! As I stepped into the huddle, I was told later that I said to the team, "Don't worry, we have this." I honestly do not remember making that statement, but all I know is that I was completely focused on winning the game.

My first pass went to Jerry for 29 yards. Next, Harold Richardson caught a pass for 11 yards, and Sam Holden caught a pass for 12 yards which gave us a first down at the Aggie 6-yard line. With less than twelve seconds left, my pass to Harold Richardson was off target. The coach sent in the next play. He called it pass 59, Jerry and I called it "Squirrel In." It was the curl route towards the back of the end zone Jerry, and I had run many times during the summer. It worked to perfection.

As I dropped back, I looked to the right for my tight end, but I felt the pocket closing in on me, so I looked and spotted Jerry in the back of the end zone. I quickly released the ball right before I got hit, and Jerry made a leaping catch to win the game. There were only four seconds left in the game when we scored. Suddenly, I felt someone picking me up and yelling, "We won, We won!" As I was turning toward the end zone, I caught a glimpse of Coach Fry flying past me headed toward the end zone to check on Jerry. Jerry was exhausted and just lying on the ground!

In the dressing room, everyone was hugging and really enjoying the victory. It was an amazing come-from-behind victory we will never forget! Coach Fry's post-game speech was extremely moving. In a very emotional voice, he reminded us that no one thought we had a chance to beat the incredibly talented team from Texas

A&M. I felt tears running down my cheek as he spoke about me and the rest of our players who had not been offered many opportunities to play in the Southwest Conference. He always joked with us about being a bunch of rag-nots but would never trade us for any other team! He praised the Aggies and their coach but bragged about us for playing like a team possessed and hungry for a victory. He ended his talk like always, with "I love you"!

After the ball game, we stopped at an excellent restaurant to eat. I cannot remember the name of the restaurant because I was too excited and too tired to even think about eating. I only remember sitting down to eat and being told by our trainer that I had a phone call. I walked to the lobby to answer the phone and quickly recognized my brother Abdon's voice. It sounded like he was struggling to talk, which made me believe that he was fighting back tears, especially when he told me Dad was so proud of me and that the whole family had watched the game. There was yelling and cheering in the background, and everyone wanted to congratulate me. After I spoke with Abdon and Senen, I spent a little time talking to a couple of other friends.

Our trainer finally told me I needed to go finish my meal so we could depart for the hotel. I was too fatigued to eat but I sure did drink lots of tea and water. What was funny about this whole thing was that going into the game I weighed 150 pounds. After the ball game I weighed 140. I lost 10 pounds in that ball game!

LIFT FOR A WINNER

outhern Methodist University Coach Hayden Fry,
ft, beams as Jerry Levias gives his hero partner.
print Inez Perez, a big lift in celebration of the

Mustangs' nerve-twanging 20-17 victory over
A&M Saturday afternoon. (See Story on Pa
AP Wirephoto.

Coach Hayden Fry, Jerry Levias and Ines celebrate
in thedressing room after their victory over Texas
A&M

Ronnie, Ines's oldest son, signaling touchdown for a

Reporter after the Texas A&M football game

Our next game was our second away game against the Missouri Tigers. Going into the Missouri game, we knew Mike Livingston was not going to play because of his injury, so it was up to Eddie Valdez and myself to do the job.

When Coach Fry announced that I would be the starter at our quarterback meeting, I knew it was going to be special. This allowed me to prove to myself and others that I could lead the team. I took 98% of the snaps during our workouts, reinforcing Coach Fry's confidence that I could handle quarterbacking the team.

Sometimes the Lord has other plans and allows us to suffer setbacks. In my case, I was injured early in the second quarter and could not finish the game.

I will never know why things play out the way they do, but one thing I do know is that God is in control of all things, and His plans are always perfect and bring glory to Him! Sure, I was disappointed, but if my setbacks will bring glory to Him and somehow help others accept Jesus as Lord and Savior, then I am okay with that.

Coach Fry did a fantastic job of preparing us for the Tigers. Our quarterback meetings were very business-like, yet fun. He had an enthusiastic sense of humor that would relax us but keep us focused. One thing the coach warned us about was hesitating or second guessing ourselves when we wanted or needed to audible at the line of scrimmage. He had tremendous confidence in us and of course we did not want to disappoint him. We really felt going into the game, we had a great game plan, and if executed right, we would win the game.

Our first series on offense was productive. Our first play of the game was supposed to be a power play off-guard, but the defensive tackle was shading to the middle, and the linebacker was tight on our guard, ready to shoot the gap. The corner towards Jerry's side rotated toward him, so that meant we had a one-on-one on our flanker, Frank Stringer. So, I audibled to a quick slant that gained twelve yards. Then the linebacker moved towards the outside, leaving the middle vulnerable to a power play, so I audibled to it. Once again, we were able to move the ball for another first down. We drove down to Missouri's thirty-four-yard line before our drive stalled. We attempted a field goal, but the ball was just slightly to the right of the goalpost.

Our defense did an excellent job of stopping the Missouri offense and forced them to punt. We got the ball with good field position and started another drive which once again ended on their twenty-seven-yard line. This time, we did not try a field goal because on a fourth and two or so, we decided to go for the first-down. A quarterback sweep was called to the short side of the field which was to my left. During summer workouts I had had good success running the quarterback sweep to the right but only once to the left.

When I took the ball, my eyes quickly fixed on the defensive end. If the end boxed across the line of scrimmage the guard was going to kick him out and I was to cut inside of his block. If the defensive end

79

squeezed inside, the guard was going to hook him, so I was to go around the end. Well, to make a long story short, the end gave me the sweep read, but he quickly jumped outside and was able to make the tackle for a one-yard gain. We did not make the first down, and Missouri took the ball over on downs.

The third series was the first series of the second quarter. We started to move the ball with a couple of good runs, but on third down, we called a bootleg. I am unsure who missed their block, but when I faked to the running back and turned around, the defensive tackle was on me. I had no chance to escape. He grabbed me around my neck and twisted me around. I was wearing long cleats for better grip in the tall grass. I could not pick up my feet because of the weight of the 300-pound tackle and my cleats being stuck in the grass. I felt every bone in my body cracking. When I tried to get up, I could not put pressure on my right leg, blood was dripping from my nose, and I was looking out the earhole of my helmet. That must have been quite a site to see for our trainers. I went back into the game a few plays later, but I could not put weight on my leg. Eddie had to finish the game for us. I felt bad for him because he had not been given many repetitions in practice, so he was limited to the offense. Undoubtedly, he could do the job because he was a tremendous athlete. He had particularly good speed and could throw the ball as well as any of us. If only he could have had more repetitions in practice. I know it would have made a significant difference.

After the game, there was no fanfare or victory celebration. Missouri had taken us to the woodshed and taught us a good lesson. We all quietly got dressed, boarded the bus, and headed to the airport for our flight home. To tell you the truth, I do not even remember having a meal after the ball game.

My interpretation upon returning to Dallas after our Missouri game is the same as the way my wife will tell it. The following is Sharron's version.

From Sharron:

"As I listened to the SMU- Missouri game on the radio, I kept cheering the team on even though no one could hear me. Ines was playing well, but SMU could not seem to get the ball across the goal line. Then the announcers were talking about Eddie Valdez playing quarterback. I did not hear any explanation of why Eddie was playing and Ines wasn't. I kept talking to the radio, telling the announcers, coaches, or anyone there to put Ines back in the game. I was so disappointed in losing the game that I got ready to go to the airport to meet the team plane when it landed. I stood in the waiting area with the fans, parents, and other players' and coaches' wives. I did not see anyone I knew, so I waited for Ines to disembark so he could tell me about the game. I waited and waited and knew there could not be any players left on the plane. The crowd had dwindled, and I could not understand why I had not seen Ines get off the plane. Then, Coach Fry's wife came over to me and introduced herself. She asked me if anyone had told me about Ines. I did not have a clue what she meant, so with a tender heart, she told me Ines had been hurt during the game. That explained a lot, but then my concern switched to Ines and his injury.

It was then I saw Ines being carried down the steps

from the plane. The trainer, Eddie Lane, told me they would take Ines to the infirmary on campus, and I could meet him there."

My version:

As we descended into Dallas, I saw a crowd outside the airport waiting for us. I could not walk on my own because of the injury, so I was told someone would carry me off the plane after everyone else had deplaned. Two of my teammates carried me off the plane and straight to Eddie's car. Eddie met with Sharron to let her know I was being taken to the infirmary. She was told to meet me there. I can just imagine what was going through Sharron's mind. All I could do was smile and blow her a kiss.

When she finally got to the infirmary, I could explain what had happened to me. She told me she was unaware I had gotten hurt during the game. Nothing was ever said about my injury. The sportscasters never mentioned I was hurt, only that Eddie was quarterbacking.

At the infirmary, we found out my leg had been wrenched, but I was told that I should be ready to play within the next two to three weeks. Sharron was visibly upset, but as a player's wife, she knew it was part of the game, and all she could do was offer her support. She was unbelievable. She helped me with my treatments and made sure I followed Eddie Lane's instructions to a "T."

The next morning, when I went to the training room to see Eddie Lane, I asked him if there was something

I could do to speed up the healing progress. Doctor Morgan happened to be there and said an injection, along with hot and cold treatments, would work wonders. I had no idea what I was getting myself into. He took out this long needle, drew a circle around the top of my ankle, and started injecting some cortisone to help relieve the pain, swelling, and irritation I was feeling in my ankle. I cannot tell you much about it because as soon as I saw puss and blood squirting everywhere, I passed out. Doctor Morgan's little boy was the next person I heard talking to me. He was asking me if I wanted the coke he was holding in his hand.

The cortisone shot certainly did what Doctor Morgan said it would. I could put weight on my foot and walk without much pain. About thirty minutes after the shot, Eddie had me enter a whirlpool full of ice. I had no way of just putting in my leg because I was bruised up to my hip, so my whole body was submerged in ice cold water. Man was it cold, but after a few seconds, I was completely numb from my shoulders down to my toes. Except for the shot, I repeated the ice treatment again at noon and once again late in the afternoon.

Sure enough, within a couple of days of hot and cold treatments three times a day I was able to put more weight on my leg. On the fourth day, I started walking up and down the stadium steps. By that afternoon, I was able to jog up a few steps. By the time our game against Minnesota rolled around on Saturday, I felt well enough to play a series or two if the coach needed me. However, I was told it would be better to give my leg a rest and not to expect to play. I traveled with the team and dressed out, but I did not play. We lost the game 23-3.

The following week we hosted Army. By then, I had fully recovered from my injury and was anticipating playing. I played a series and quickly drove the team down for a score. We lost to the Army 24-6.

The following week we went to Houston to play Rice. Traditionally the SMU vs Rice game was always a close game, and this one was no different. It did not disappoint anyone. Our defense was playing lights out, but Rice took advantage of our mistake and beat us 14-10. That was pretty much the way the whole season went. We would play great for fifty-nine minutes, but somehow, the last minute seemed to be our downfall. Our season did not go well, and we ended with a 3-7 record.

I need to add that during the season, we lost nine defensive and seven offensive players to injuries. We finally got all our players back from injuries for the last two games of the season. Our next to last game we beat Baylor 16-10 and finished the season by beating TCU 28-14.

Getting the chance to start against Missouri was particularly special. I could not help but think that I could help our team defend our conference championship. But sometimes, the Lord has other plans and allows us to experience setbacks. Not only did we lose the game, but I also suffered an injury that pretty much ended my season.

We must realize that what God wants and needs to accomplish through us is far more important than playing in a football game or participating in any other activity.

His goal is for us to share the gospel of our Lord Jesus Christ through the platform he has provided us. For me, having had national exposure provided me with opportunities to speak at banquets and FCA meetings. Through our Coaches Outreach Bible Studies, the door has been opened to coaches, both men and women, to learn and model Christ-like characteristics.

I mentioned Tommy Maxwell's name when we played A&M as an outstanding football player; what I did not know was that he later became an ordained minister. It is funny how God brings Christian brothers together for His Glory.

Tommy and I met officially at an Aggie gathering. A friend of mine, who graduated from A&M, invited me to what he called a small gathering of Aggies. Little did I know that it was not a small gathering; it was a big meet the "Aggies" type picnic.

Word got around that I was at the picnic, so Tommy came over to speak to me. My heart started pumping, and I just knew he was going to hit me in the mouth. However, he introduced himself, and I found out he did not come over to fight but to greet me. He was very cordial and receptive towards me being there.

It did not take long for me to see and feel Tommy's heart. He told me about his ministry in Georgetown, Texas, and how God was leading him toward something different. He said he had an idea of starting a Bible study for coaches. I thought it was a terrific idea and encouraged him to do so. He mentioned he had also talked to Tommy

Cox, another outstanding football player and coach in the Central Texas area. Before long, Tommy Maxwell had several coaches attending a Bible study at the Texas High Coaches Association office.

Eddie Joseph, former athletic director of the Texas High School Coaches Association, hosted coaches on Thursdays from Round Rock (myself, Larry Hirt, Leonard McAngus, Nic Nichols), Bowie High School (Tommy Cox, Andy Jackson, Tom Hancock, David Seaborn), and Ron Schroeder, Head Coach at Westlake High School. This group has been instrumental in empowering coaches through the "Coaches Outreach Bible Studies."

Tommy Maxwell, Tommy Cox, and the Coaches Outreach Bible Studies have not only brought Jesus into the lives of local coaches, but these studies have expanded to several other states. Without a doubt, Coaches Outreach has been a blessing to hundreds of coaches, athletes, and parents.

Exodus 15:2, a scripture Sister Mary taught us in Catechism jumped out at me; it reads: "The Lord is my strength and my defense; he has become my salvation. He is my God, and I will praise him, my father's God, and I will exalt Him." (NIV)

LETTERFROM LOVED ONES

LETTER FROM MARCOS G. PEREZ

NOVEMBER 9, 2023

A TRIBUTE TO INES PEREZ: BY MARCOS G. PEREZ

INES PEREZ BECAME A POPULAR TEXAS HIGH SCHOOL FOOTBALL LEGEND BEGINNING AT ROY MILLER HIGH SCHOOL IN CORPUS CHRISTI, TEXAS. NOT ONLY DID INES BECAME A UIL ALL-STATE QUARTERBACK, BUT HE ALSO WAS INSTRUMENTAL IN LEADING THE SCHOOL BASEBALL TEAM TO THE REGIONAL PLAYOFFS.

WHILE I WAS AT A LARGE GATHERING PARTY, SEVERAL PEOPLE SHARED WITH ME THAT BECAUSE OF INES' HIGH SCHOOL

ACCOMPLISHMENTS, YOUNG ATHLETES AROUND THE CITY OF CORPUS CHRISTI WOULD GO AROUND TELLING THEIR FRIENDS, WHILE PLAYING SANDLOT FOOTBALL, THAT THEY WERE GOING TO BE THE NEXT INES PEREZ. SO, NOT ONLY WAS INES PEREZ A GREAT ATHLETE, BUT HE WAS ALSO A ROLE MODEL FOR MANY FUTURE HIGH SCHOOL ATHLETES. IN ADDITION TO THE ABOVE

ACHIEVEMENTS, INES ACCOMPLISHED MANY OTHER ACCOLADES WHICH OUR FAMILY KNEW THAT "ONLY THROUGH THE GRACE OF GOD" COULD INES HAVE REACHED HIGH LEVELS OF GOALS

WHICH INCLUDE PLAYING IN THE UIL SOUTH ALL-STAR FOOTBALL GAME; NOMINATED AS AN ALL-AMERICAN QUARTERBACK AT HENDERSON JR. COLLEGE; NAMED "BACK OF THE WEEK' AT SMU WHILE

DEFEATING TEXAS A&M IN 1967; FURTHERMORE, INES PLAYED IN THE JR. COLLEGE ROSE BOWL; PLAYED

IN THE SOUTHWEST CONFERENCE COTTON BOWL, JANUARY 1ST, 1968; MOREOVER, INES WAS A

SUCCESSFUL HIGH SCHOOL FOOTBALL
COACH AND ATHLETIC DIRECTOR FOR OVER
30 YEARS. WAS HE

BLESSED OR WHAT? SOME PEOPLE MAY
THINK THAT INES' MANY
ACCOMPLISHMENTS MAY NOT BE SO

GREAT; BUT WHEN PEOPLE BECOME AWARE
THAT INES COMPETED WHEN HE WAS ONLY
5'4" AND 14O

LBS., PEOPLE BECOME SILENT, SEEM
SURPRISED, AND CAN'T BELIEVE HOW
DIMINUTIVE INES WAS AND

WAS ABLE TO BECOME A SUCCESSFUL
ATHLETE AT HIS DIMUNUTIVE SIZE. ONCE
AGAIN, OUR PARENTS

ALWAYS REMINDED ALL OF US (FAMILY
MEMBERS), THROUGH THE GRACE OF GOD,
ONE CAN

ACCOMPLISH ANYTHING IF IT'S IN HIS WILL-
ALL WE HAVE TO DO IS ASK AND PRAY FOR
GOD'S WILL.

IN ADDITION, OUR PARENTS' DISCLAIMER
WAS IF WHATEVER YOU ASK FOR DOESN'T
HAPPEN, GOD WILL HAVE ANOTHER PLAN
FOR US. OUR FAMILY FEELS BLESSED OF

HAVING INES AS OUR YOUNGER BROTHER
AND THAT THE BLESSINGS HE RECEIVED
MAY HAVE BEEN BECAUSE WE WERE
BLESSED TO HAVE BLESSED PARENTS WHO
GUIDED US AND SUPPORTED EVERYONE
"THROUGH THE GRACE OF GOD.

MARCOS G. PEREZ 3RD THE OFFSPRING IN
THE FAMILY OF 4 BOTHERS AND 3 SISTERS.

LETTER FROM BEST FRIEND

Ines Perez and I established a lifelong friendship at the age of 12 or 13 while playing little league baseball. By the 8th grade, our love for baseball shifted to football. From the 9th grade up to our sophomore year, we both worked extremely hard to get stronger and faster. We played together on a team that played for the State Championship, losing to Garland from Dallas, Texas. We then played in Junior College for the Henderson County "Cardinals" and were fortunate to play on a Conference Championship team that played in the "Junior Rose Bowl" in Pasadena, California. Our lasting friendship escalated from friends to almost brothers. During my teenage years, I was either at my house or at the Perez's, visiting or lifting weights. His older brother, Senen was my primary mentor. After leaving Henderson County Junior College, we accepted scholarships to different schools.

I wish we could have stayed together but the good Lord haddifferent plans for us, however, we remain as close as brothers.

Alfred Boyd

LETTER FROM TRINI LOPEZ

September 26, 198?

Dear Inez:

Just a note to say that I hope your feeling
better and that all is going well for you
after the setback.

It was a real thrill to hear that you had been
given the nickname of "TRINI" ....what an honor
for me.

I look forward to the time that we can meet and
spend some time together. I'll be in Dallas
toward the end of December, I hope you'll have
a little time then.

With best wishes and warmest regards.

Sincerely,

TRINI LOPEZ

Inez Perez
"TRINI"
SMU Athletic Department
Dallas, Texas 75222

LETTER FROM PETE RAGUS

The Mighty Mite
By Pete Ragus   1

In my 37 year career as a coach and athletic director I had the privilege of knowing and dealing with thousands of athletes with outstanding attitudes, great work ethic, and each of them was unique in his or her own way. It was such an honor for me to be a part of so many outstanding lives.

But there is one athlete, out of these thousands of athletes, that stands out in his uniqueness. He is Ives Perez who was Quarterback on our 1963 state finalist Miller High School football Team. Ives led Miller to the state championship game, when all the facts about Ives said this cannot happen, it is impossible. Here are the facts that said this is impossible. Ives was 5'3" tall. They said he can't see or throw over the linemen. He weighed 129 pounds, they said he was not tough enough and he would be crushed. they said he had little hands, how can he possibly throw the ball.

In spite of these facts, what the 1963 Team accomplished, under his leadership, was absolutely amazing. The team was state finalist, and in 60 years no other Team south of San Antonio has done this. this team beat some of the states best Teams of that era. the Team was not favored in each of these games. they beat San Antonio Brackenridge with Warren McVey, San Antonio

2

Lee with Linus bear, and Spring Branch with Chris Gilbert. They played an amazing and historic game against Kingsville for the district championship, the day President Kennedy was assassinated.

What Ines accomplished at Miller was against all reason for a quarterback of his size, but there are more amazing things to come in his life.

They said surely he can't play in college with those big linemen. He did not get any division one college offers, so he went to Henderson Junior College.

So what does this too small young man, who should not be able to play in college accomplish at Henderson. He led Henderson to the National Championship game that was played in the Rose Bowl in Pasadena California. They lost that game but they were finalist. Now all of that is too amazing to be true, but there is more amazing things to come.

Surely any reasonable person would say he can't do division one football. But Hayden Fry at SMU was keeping up with Ines's accomplishments and he gave him a scholarship at SMU. He was basically a back up quarterback, but he made national news and Time magazine when he came into a game

against A+M on national T.V. I was
fortunately watching the game. The starting
quarterback got hurt and Ines came in
while SMU was behind. Ines led smu
to victory with a pass to Jerry Levias in
the end zone. Ines made National sports
news and had a picture in Time magazine
with the statement under the picture,
"quarterback in a hole," he could barely see
over the center. All of this was truly one
of the most memorable and joyous moments
in my life. He proved he could play division
one football.

Ines was also a young man of deep
faith and I am sure this was a big
part in making him who he was and is.

In my opinion, because his life was so
amazing, unique, and so far of the norm
of what coaches look for in a quarterback,
a movie should ~~should~~ be made of his
life. IT would not only be a great movie,
but more importantly it would be an
inspiration To young people and all people,
that regardless of your handicaps and
circumstances you can accomplish something.

LETTER TO CORRINA ROGERS

To Corrina Rogers

I am especially grateful for all the time, effort, and wisdom she provided me the past few weeks in making sure I met deadlines, spelled words correctly, and connected all the information with the time and period being communicated.

I'm grateful for all the advice and expertise provided throughout the entire process. It made writing this book much easier. However, most of all, I appreciate the patience she had with me, I know it was not easy!

Thank you, Corrina

LETTER FROM SHARRON

When I was a student at Henderson County Junior College, I, like everyone else on campus, knew who Ines Perez was. I went to all the home games and thought he was a great quarterback. I never gave much thought to getting to know him, much less marrying him!

Most of the students at HCJC rode buses every day, but I lived in the dorm. The girls' dorm was a split level, with the main level being "upstairs" and stairs. There were only four rooms. Needless to say, the eight of us girls living downstairs became good friends. Two of the girls were cheerleaders and knew who all the football players were. Most of us were protestant, but two of the girls were Catholic. All of us were talking one day about our religion and our faith and since the protestant girls had never been to a Catholic mass, we were curious. So, we were invited to go with them to mass on Valentine's Day.

We got rides to the Catholic Church in Athens because it wasn't within walking distance. During mass, we could see some of the football players sitting close to the front and got a good look at them when they went for communion. I thought Ines was very cute, but I thought he was focused on the mass.

When we returned to the campus, we went to the cafeteria for lunch, the final meal served on Sundays. While we were eating, some of my friends interacted with the football players who had come in.

When I got back to the dorm, my friends said Ines wanted to meet me. Talk about total shock! The plan was for some of us girls and some of the football players to walk together to the convenience store later in the afternoon for snacks. On our way back from the store Ines asked me to sit on the steps of the Student Union Building with him.

I enjoyed our visit and I thought he was very nice. He asked about how I had grown up and where I went to high school, and I found out about him. I thought it was a typical girl meets boy type conversation. When he walked me back to the dorm, he told me he was going to marry me. Well, that was "straight out of left field!" I could not say anything except, "You're crazy!"

We continued to see each other and he kept telling me he was going to marry me. I grew to like him enough that I was beginning to really believe him. Needless to say, "liking" turned into "loving" and he asked me to marry him.

Getting married while we were in college was not easy on either of us. Since we didn't have any money, I lived with his family for the spring semester, 1966, while he finished his last semester of junior college. When he left for SMU, I went with him. Then life really became interesting.

We were expecting a baby by then and I needed to work. I found out what real work was all about with a baby to care for and working full time; all while trying to help Ines anyway I could.

Ines' life wasn't easy either. He had to study hard to maintain his grades while keeping up with his training, workouts, team meetings and games. And, he worked part-time when he could.

God was a constant in our lives because we couldn't have made it to his graduation without God guiding our way. We made sure to go to church every Sunday and teach our children about Jesus Christ.

Ines has been a wonderful husband and a great father to our five children. He adores our 12 grandchildren and takes pride in our great-grandchildren (at this time we have eleven great-grands!)

I'm truly blessed!

TO GOD BE THE GLORY

WIN, WIN, WIN, HEY!!!

Made in the USA
Monee, IL
27 November 2024

71447842R00062